LIKE THE
PALM TREES SWAY
LOVE POEMS

Lauren Eden

LIKE THE
PALM TREES SWAY
LOVE POEMS

Lauren Eden

LIKE THE PALM TREES SWAY

Self-published by Lauren Eden
laureneden.me

Cover photo: David Hall

ISBN: 978-0-6489872-2-2

P O E M S

For my Henry:
the embodiment of love.
You're food and drink to me.

PALM READER

I trace California in my palm.
Map the 405 heading to the 105.
Mark the Palos Verdes Hills
arching over my love line.

Sweeping the flat sands of Hermosa Beach
leading to blue sea veins,
I feel the tickle of joy swim like fish
up through the golden ring of
Saturn. Sticking his middle finger
up at the world, he knows it is he
who is the ruler of fate.

I follow him, and you are there,
if only a little late. Swinging in
the white moon of my thumbnail
like a hammock. Arms behind your head.
You. Right at my fingertips.

BACKBONE

I am with you. Your fingerprints
ink my skin. Matching
the ones within. Touched
before you had touched me.

Six months of conversations
coil around my wrists. I have not one
on my tongue—I am ill-prepared.
I just want to be kissed!
I've waited three decades for you.

I kiss you first. You giggle.
This is joy: the way your hands hold
the arch of my back
like it's never been broken.

THE KISS
(Italic lines: "The Kiss" by Anne Sexton)

My mouth blooms like a cut.
It is yours that heals it.
Between the cotton sheets of our
beachside-rental bed: you, me, and poetry
folded like a dog-eared page.

This is the fairy tale.
White marshmallow pillows
propping my jet-lagged head.
Clutching your arm as you read
the way a child clutches her father
before they cross a busy street.

Before today my body was useless.
An apple seed wasted in the pit of my stomach.
I feel my organs opening to orchards.

You sharpen your American r's on Anne Sexton.
I cut my ears on each word tea*rrrrr*ing across the page,
slicing open the air like scissors through gift wrap.
Will your kiss be this sharp?
I'm willing to find out.

I kiss you first. You taste like blood
dried from an old wound —
or is this new?
I can't be held accountable
for what my hunger makes me do.

I've been sitting on it for years, like birds
waiting for something to crack.

My nerves are turned on.
I hear them like musical instruments.
I fall into your hours, like our kiss.

Love, love you are on time.
Just not on my watch.

COSMIC COUPLING

Travelling toward San Jacinto,
our fingers braid together as you drive,
weaving in and out like the long hair of a schoolgirl.

Bush sunflowers on the side of the road
turn in the breeze like clock dials.
I read aloud our horoscope to kill time.
Delighting in the 'delightful degradations'
of the cosmic coupling
between your sun sign and mine:
the Scorpio dominant, the Cancer submissive.
The black bat, the pink bunny.
More accoutrements in the bedroom
than all the porn studios in San Fernando Valley.

You grinned. I squeezed my legs tight.
Our constellations spiralling
in the moving shadows
across my thighs—and if the forecast is wrong,
never mind.
We always have our moons.

CROW

It wasn't until night-time I saw it: the poem
coiled inside your left eye like a snake.
You sat opposite me at dinner. Conversations about
the acute degrees of love-trigonometry sitting between us
like our glasses of chilled white.
Each sip unravelling the loose lips of that tightly scrolled line.
Did you know what was written? I couldn't make it out.
I knew I'd have to get closer to you.
Much closer.

Leaning forward in my chair, I listened to you speak.
My head in my hands, trying to read your fine print.
Something about joy. Whitman?
No, *darker*. Something ominous. Something more like Hughes.
Black feathered font like the wings of a crow.
Razor-tipped serifs. Double-edged entendre. *Crow-speak.*
That's what you were: A crow.
A bad omen to a woman who'd never died before,
but to one who already had?
You were a prophecy.

You blinked and the poem disappeared,
falling into the black hole of your pupil.
I hid my sigh inside my sip.

Whatever was written,
there was one thing I knew for certain:
it was no fortune cookie.

BERMUDA

'I love the way your hips hang on you,'
you say, as though they were a dress.

You draw a triangle of my hip bones with your
index finger. *Bermuda*.
Get lost in me. Never come up for air!
Many a love-drunk sailor has disappeared in my
wreckage of bones. In some reflections of sea, I've been Siren,
sometimes Scylla,
depending on their shade of blue,
depending on the concentration of my salt.

Whispering wonder at the geometry of nature:
in nautilus shells, in honey, in flowers,
you put the triangle of my hip in your mouth —
the hips that have swallowed men,
now swallowed by your lips.

Lifting my arms above my head, you free me
from my dress.
There are no walls between us.
No countries, no oceans, no screens,
only fabric. Thin cotton blue.

'God,' you say. Once.
Gratefully. As though you finally understood
the punishment of clothes.

AMERICAN BOY

He drives on the other side of the road.
I should've known he would fuck me differently,
this American boy.
I think I moaned in reverse.

SATURN RETURNS

I've chased you for two hundred thousand years.
It explains the taper above my hips.
My psychedelic trips.
I've run circles around you in my sleep.

You say 'sit down' when I lean above you.
My shirt pulled over my head
(I'm in over my head)
and it sounds like Saturn. *Sat-urn.*
The memory of you returning,
like the rings I sway around you.

Dizzy and head-spun, I kiss your
wet mouth another time.
'Hello stranger,' I say with a smile.
'How nice of you to return to me.'

MINI-SKIRT MILITANT

Peace came when I did. Ironically,
with your hand around my neck
in my white-sheet surrender.

Slowly I'd been unpicking myself from my battles
since the day you arrived.
Hair by hair, finger by finger.
Peeling my wounds away like stickers.

Sleepy-limbed and out of fight, I sent my soldiers home.
Told them my war was over.
Then I kissed you and I kissed you
like that famous wartime photograph
of an American sailor kissing a nurse in Times Square
with glee.

The war is over. The gloves are off.
My hands are in your hair.

SCRAPBUK

Side by side, we ripped up
your Bukowski books,
while sitting cross-legged on the floor
in our underwear.

There was a tenderness we saw in Buk
we both begged stay a little longer.
A soft wilting rose of vulnerability
found growing between his thorny tales
of horse-racing and whores.
Fancying ourselves his best editor,
we vowed to put together his best anthology of delicacies:
'Confession.' 'Bluebird.' 'Raw With Love.'

I almost cried, you almost cried,
as we ripped each page slowly from its spine,
like two brats pulling the wings off a fly.

'I feel like I'm going to go to Hell for this,'
I said, watching you watch me rip up
your *Burning in Water, Drowning in Flame* first edition.

You shrugged, accepting our fate.
'Maybe you can grab a beer with Buk
when you get there.'

NAVAJO

With voices raspy from sleep, we take turns
to read *Birthday Letters* on the sofa
between sips of espresso. If mornings can be perfect,
this one is perfection.
Startlingly so.

You mistake my hand on the page for your own.
Lines flowing from our mouths like seas
lapping up each other's accents: your r's hard,
mine soft, like syllabic roses with their thorns
hacked off.

Nothing in this country sounds the same.
The sky filled with unfamiliar birdsong.
The nights throbbing with strange siren sounds.
The only thing familiar is this feeling:
I love you
and you love me
in ways I've always known.
It comes back to me in waves. Like the way
your tongue moves in your mouth
when you teach me how to pronounce *Navajo.*

LOOM

I did not expect you'd come. Loom-spun,
I'd hung up my dreams over the back of my chair
facing the window. I thought if they must fade,
let it be by light. It is the purest rival.

I'd left my door open, which was odd in itself,
but in truth, by then I feared nothing.
I saw you from my window first, watching you
stumble through the vineyard, more drunk on beauty
than liquor. Your lips, the wildest red.
Was it from blood or the wine?
The memory is interchangeable.

I knew who you were by who you reminded me of.
Somebody I wanted to forget.
Somebody with that same complicated head that tied me
up in knots. That same cold shoulder, colder than the moon.
It dug up graves. I had no more flowers.

'Do you think we keep falling in love
with the same person all our lives?'
'Yes,' you replied. 'Over and over, and we get better at it.'

Maybe you were right, maybe you weren't.
All I knew was I wanted to get better.
So up I lifted my arms to the sky, and like a sweater,
you put my dreams back over my head.

X I X

Wilted and wept, I faced your sun.
That burning fireball in your chest
tongue-lashing with colour.

I knew not of what the earth you burned for.
If you burned for any one thing but for what lived
inside you. I needed no permission.
Rolling my paths into serpent coils, I took off
my shoes. I sat under you.
Confetti of orbs celebrated your light.

Hovering over me, I wrote your name
between every stroke of shadow across
my skin. You put my pen down,
then wiped the world from my eyes like sleep.

I woke up in you. My life spiralling into
the black hole of my blind spot
as I stared. Seeing nothing but your light
boring through my pupils like a corkscrew.

I stared until I could see through you.
I stared until I could see through the sun.

EM DASH

I never once saw a comma.
You wrote how you spoke: swift and exact like Cupid.
You loved, or you didn't.

Once you apologised for it
the way one apologises for a kink in their personality
they have no intention of ironing out,
like a penchant for laughing when they're in trouble,
or arriving late to every party
so they're never the first to arrive.

I never once saw a comma.
Not a quick draw of air—only em dashes
like empty beds we'd lie on after eating too many words,
lying on our backs holding our stomachs
in pregnant pause.

You loved how you wrote:
without hesitation; no breaths.
A sentence ended or it began.
You opened your mouth to speak,
or you closed it.

You loved with the grandest poetic declarations,
or else, you read.

Lauren Eden

BLISS

If there is something I've been keeping from myself,
it is this: this bliss.

Lying on my back on the white fur rug
giggling. You, smiling down on me
like sunlight.

And I don't quite know where it's coming from:
all this *light* —
the sun in my chest,
or the one I'm looking at.

TESTAMENT
Homage to "Testament: Homage to Walt Whitman" by Erica Jong.

The Palm Springs mountains loom
like a cardboard cut-out scene.
Two lovers pasted on the patio.
The other guests cut out. Uninvited.

My legs stretch out on the sun lounge,
glossy with desert heat. This Summer, I vow to wear
only the sun and you.
I know no difference in my sweat.

Reading Erica Jong aloud, I read you my favourite lines.
My toes saluting the sun like worshippers with tonsure.
Drinking your morning coffee, you recite
the run-on sentences of my legs for your memory.

We speak of Erica's awakening:
from 1970s feminist machete
to Walt Whitman's gardener
cutting his *Leaves of Grass.*
How all women soften eventually.

I 'declare myself now for joy,' I read.
Triumphantly.
I declare myself for you.

NEON

I am *obsessed* with you
we exclaim in between
fistfuls of hair and
fits of giggles, giddy
with big loud neon love.

HOW TO LOVE:

1. Close your eyes and imagine your chest is the sun.
2. Sweat.

B L U R

There is something about you
that makes me want to forget
every damn thing I've learned about love
and come to you dumb and gentle
with hands softer than snow,
melting into you a blur of myself
never fighting for my outline,
never fighting at all.

COSMIC

It reminds me of Saturn.
The smooth planetary tip
my tongue runs rings around.

An orbit of licks slowing time,
dancing in your diamond rain.

There might not be life on Mars,
but on Saturn?
There is no question.

DADDY

Like a basket of spoiled fruit, I sit in your lap
showing you my skinned knees,
showing you where I still bleed
from that wound you can see on days like these:
when the sun parts the sea a little too far to the left
and all the blue falls in.

In your hammock of hands, I sway
back and forth without release.
I've dreamt my entire life
for a man who feels like sleep.

If I had been birthed by a man, I could imagine
it would've been by you. *My god.*
A thick cord from plexus to plexus
flexing and loosening
as I move on you like a sigh.

And if you didn't make me so wet,
I might call you 'Daddy'
because you are the only man
who's ever felt like home.

A SIMPLE KALEIDESCOPE

The sky turns orange
my hips turn pink
as you grip me
against the windowsill.

I see a California sunset.
I see palm trees.
Then I see stars.

WIKILEAKS

I tell them how I fell for you.
Swallowing my own lies
the way I eat peas: gulped down fast
with a slosh of bravado.

I didn't *fall* for you.
I dripped.

VITAL

You trickled through me like blood.
My veins pricked open like cat ears,
alert to the surprise of you filling me.

I thought you'd feel like pleasure.
Instead, you felt vital.

S U N F L O W E R S
(Lyric: "Break on Through (To the Other Side) by The Doors)

'I found an island in your arms. Country in your eyes,'
you hum The Doors as you pull
my Jim Morrison t-shirt over my head
lyrically, then fumble with the silver button on my
jeans, my hips lifting to the lilt of your rhyme
to keep the moment musical.

We're not the sharp corners type:
pointed elbows, jutting-hip hesitations.
We are dreamers!
Two dreamers with the same dream.
A wave that chooses direction once
then flows. Sex never letting go of its grasp
until our soft-mouthed kiss opens to a gasp.

I watch you like a cat in your afterglow:
eyes dazed at the ceiling, the stars in your head.
I have never been this close to art before.
I look at your bare chest next to mine returning to its rhythm,
wondering where you keep it.
It seems to be everywhere.
Plath on your fingertips.
Sexton on your cut red mouth.
Morrison, an asp, coiled inside your chest.
Nin on your cock.

Keeping my chin at your chin,
I watch your eyes like changing canvases.

Once I saw a Van Gogh painting in your eyes
when you fucked me. Your hands,
a vase around my neck.
Two sunflower irises aflame.
Fuzzy black pupils.

It was hard not to touch them.
To resist plucking those beautiful hints of madness
from their stems,
before your stroke of sanity revealed
a pentimento field of empty vision.
But only for a moment. Only until you looked at me again.
Then as before, the whole mad world bloomed
in your eyes.

YANG

There is nothing sexier than a man's strength.
There is nothing more terrifying.

VITRUVIAN MAN

We woke naked in the shape of a wheel.
Our backs flat on the bed on opposite ends.
One body: a bud fallen open in flower.

Four arms, four legs extended out
like a compass that had all the world covered.

My head chose north.
Your head chose south.
The equator travelling across the middle
of our still-joined pelvises.
The Atlantic running down my leg.

Da Vinci never drew a woman for the Vitruvian man.
Her legs slung wide over his bare muscular shoulders,
and if he had,
maybe he would be in colour.

CONFETTI

Like confetti.
That's how you throw love.
You worry about the mess tomorrow.

THE PROPOSAL

Putting a rubber ring around his cock
he asked me if I'd like to,
you know.

I sighed and said, 'I do.'
I do, I do, I do.

PLAYING HOUSE

A poet needs a lover, not a spouse.
Still, that didn't stop us playing house
in a small beach bungalow down the road
from the apartment you shared with
your girlfriend.

It took seven days to create a new world.
On the eighth, we created Heaven.
The refrigerator humming 'Hallelujah'
as we made gods out of each other under the halo
of your *Coastal Living* inspired candlelight.

The coffee machine poured good mornings
in lipstick-stained mugs insisting goodnight.
Your ironed work-shirts hung up in the wardrobe
like paintings waiting to dry. On the coffee table
sat the keys to your residence: your real home —
reminding me this domestic dream was only on loan
like a library book I'd return late,
my favourite pages ripped out.

On the last day I saw you reading with a furrowed brow.
It was the most serious I'd seen you all week,
for there were no bills to pay
except for the damage we left at home
that we would be paying for longer than we could've known.

When the week ended, we split our assets.
You got the caramel scented candles,
the Bukowski scrapbook
and I, our stuffed cat.

The judge and jury ordering poetry
as alimony.
You are overdue.

ELEMENTAL

I was supposed to be your fire.
Your passion. The warmth
you'd been craving.
Thick syrupy Death Valley heat.

Not your water. Not your air.
Not your zen Japanese Garden.
Not your lullaby Santa Monica breeze.
No, you were not expecting that

all the elements would rise
from my hair. That I would be
balanced. Symmetrical.
A globe steady on its axis.

That I would be everything:
the world, and yours.

SCARLET A

My suitcase on the bed:
flung open like your mouth
the night before on me.
Munch's *Scream.*

I will ache in all the places
my body dipped into yours
as it slept. I will change shape.

Pulling me into you,
your eyes studded with tears
like chesterfield couches only fit for Henry Miller,
you say, 'Thank you —
for being brave.'

I smile. A glint like money in my eye.
If all women behaved,
there'd have been no Anaïs Nin.

CRIMINAL

The infinity symbol: a tired pink bow
on the front of my knickers
frazzled at the ends like our goodbye
rushed and half-realised
at the terminal.

Security stops me at checkpoint.
My crime: smuggling yellow light
down the front pocket of my overalls.
The guard pointing at the monitor
revealing an aura of luminescence
fanning through my chest.

I stole your heart.
I am a criminal.

P O P

Nothing is the same after that first goodbye.
You were loving inside a bubble.
Now you're loving on the edge of a pin.

OLD GUM

My memories of you have lost their flavour
like old gum I've been chewing on for days.

Ruminating on your spearmint kiss,
the sea of your mouth
snaking and wet down the back of my neck,
now dry.

They taste like defeat.
Like corked wine, like long goodbyes.
I taste only me.

FERAL

We scratch at our phone screens.
Two stray cats feral from neglect,
mad with the memory of milk.

IDOLATRY

Don't let them tell you:
you can't make idols out of lovers.

Lovers more god than human.
Lovers with hearts made of broken pieces of star
embedded and threaded in their chests.

Fuck. You can get down on your knees
and let the worms crawl in your hair
if the one you love has feet more beautiful
than the souls and the soles of all the men
who walked before him.

Your worship wearing his skin to bone,
until you feel God dripping out of him.

GLASS

I put off showering the way I put off a hard conversation:
squirming in my skin
one foot out, the other in
eyes on the exit
wrapped up in a warm fluffy towel of procrastination.

I do not want this man off my skin!
I want to be Cleopatra mummified in his bedsheets.
An artefact of his sexual history.
If I shall bathe, let it be in *him*.
A Roman bath of his blood, sweat and cum.

Scrubbing your fingerprints off my skin like I'm getting you off
with my murder,
I watch your kisses flake like dead skin
sliding down the drain with my tears.
The evidence rolls off my back like surf.
You pool at my feet.

The screen fogs like grief.
I break into a giggle. This is *absurd*
how much it hurts
to miss someone so much that water
can feel like glass.

Lauren Eden

LIKE THE PALM TREES SWAY

Running two blocks to talk to me,
a man spotted me on the other side of the street,
my hips swaying like the palm trees sway.

Out of breath, he looked at me with awe
like I was dripping in liquid gold.
Dude, it's sex.
My legs have been open for seven days.
I've been filled from sun to moon. Fucked
like I was a portal into every man's wet
teenage dream.

Is there a me on the other side of me?
I saw her today on the other side of the street,
her hips swaying like the palm trees sway.
Love multiplying me.

PLAGIARIST

God. My lover. Are you a thing to miss.
I plagiarise your touch by day. Sit on my hands
at night. It is a crime they'd even try
to touch myself the way that you do.
Flimsy fingered fools! Who do they think they're kidding?
I know all their tricks.
If only they knew yours.

How I need to not know what's coming,
like the sudden slap across my arse
or the fourth hard yank of my hair
when I could barely bear the third, but this is harder to:
knowing I can't surprise myself. My hand diving
down under, pink flamingo nails
snatching my precious ocean pearl.
It's so *feminine.* So dainty. It's no good.
I hate my girlishness.

But *you*—your touch is genius.
It's brutal brilliance. A masterpiece,
my violent virtuoso. And I am just a kid
finger-painting,
trying to replicate art.

ARGUING OVER SHADES OF BLACK

The cracks were bigger when I met you.
Is that facetious of me to say?
You fell in hard and often.
I'd hear the thud like a bag of coal on a Sunday night.
Just Friday, you were a balloon.

Now I barely hear a sound.
That's not to say it doesn't echo.
That it still doesn't hurt for you to crawl into
your cuts—but tell me you can't see
how this new world of ours is only pixelated
into millions of greyscale moods. Rarely any of them black.
It is an illusion.

The black coat of a sleeping Bombay turning to rust in the sun.
Coming back from a trip to the dark side of the moon
with a colourful souvenir: the violet bruise between my legs
I spotted in the shower the day I came home from my week
with you and played Amy Winehouse's 'Back to Black'
back-to-back on repeat fifteen times in an hour,
crying every time she sang: 'You go back to her,
and I go back to black,' on a loop, like a noose
stringing myself up with my sadness.

That day, I knew black,
like a cat knows its own tail,
and no one—not even you
could argue it was onyx.

METAMOUR

It sounds romantic. French.
Metamour. She is my metamour.
The woman on the other side of the man I love.
Call it: his head or tail?

The woman who stands between us.
Sometimes over. Sometimes with her back turned,
like a fly that's on a different wall
every time I look.

The biggest thing we have in common is
you, but I've heard she likes cats,
so maybe there are more.
Not that it's our commonalities you like most.
You like our differences. You like us exotic.

On a good day, she and I
are like a pear and an apple on the same tree.
A mushy fruit salad on the worst day,
depending on the angle of the breeze.
Depending on how hard the branch shakes
when one of us sneezes.

Each month, I think of texting her:
Are we on the same cycle? Are we syncing?
Because it seems it's always on the same day
we both ask you: 'So, tell me, are we sinking?'

VICKY CRISTINA CALIFORNIA

Last year she gave him a new surfboard
for his birthday.

This year, she gave him me.

THE GIRL WHO CRIED WOLF

First, I cried,
and then I came
to the thought of you
in bed with her.

If the worst thing
that can come out of this
is an orgasm,

I am living in fear
of all the wrong things.

LAST SEASON

They know your name like Summer and Spring.
Like Fall. They know it all.
Everything that trickles from me.
Everything I can't keep in.

To know you is to know me.
Keeping you a secret will keep me a secret.
An outdated version of myself sitting at their table
talking over coffee about love
as though I ever knew a thing about it.

I would be a liar.
And I gave up lying in the Winter.

ETERNAL SUMMER

We will pass the sun between our mouths
like an orange Skittle. Swap seasons
like baseball cards. Steal summers
from my corner to yours like delinquents
misbehaving for the love of it.

Your hand on the back of my neck will never
get cold—I'll will it burn.
Our skin will stay as brown as picked berries,
and we will keep each other close
despite the heat between us,
but because of it.

Flowers know the kind of climate they will bloom in.
Lovers are no different.

IT SOMETIMES RAINS IN SOUTHERN CALIFORNIA

It's been four months; we try to play it cool.
End up making love when we don't intend to
in the stay before the stay:
a Travelodge ten minutes from LAX.
I'd been up in the air all night.
The prospect of touching you soon couldn't be.

I'd promised you I was going to drip all over you
but the ceiling has me covered.
A raindrop falls for your left cheek, getting to you first.
A kiss from Santa Ana. You laugh,
wiping it away with your sleeve.
I am jealous.

Albert Hammond knew shit.
It seems sometimes it does rain in Southern California.

CAR CRASH

One. Two. Three.
We count car crashes on the freeway
on our way to brunch in San Bernardino.
'Sunday morning,' I offered simply.
The most dangerous time to drive.
People are still drunk, people are sad —
and that was how you preferred it:
driving headfirst into the cusp of Saturday night paradise
spiralling rapidly into Sunday morning hell.

It was the hope you loved, but the hopelessness
that moved you.
The light in people's eyes that flicker on
then off. Faulty-bulbed souls that don't know
if their purpose is darkness or light.
Whether they are suns or moons.

'Don't look,' you said.
I kept my eyes on you.

You, looking once in the rear-view mirror,
then again for the both of us.

NEPTUNE

We met in deep waters.
The blue lifted to the surface like tea leaves.
This was beyond mood.

I found you in the dark. I felt you first.
Spellbound before I knew your stories and that
spirited way you tell them.
The sea swam around our shape: our dark degrees
of Neptune. Holding our golden trident
we tried to bend into a triangle so nobody
would get hurt.

I remind myself each day where we met.
What colour the sky was.
The way we ran to our corners. Bookended
by the same blues.

I found you in the dark.
You: my feathered thing.

I learned that just because a thing is dark,
it doesn't mean that it will hurt you.

LIFT-OFF

Gazing skyward,
her small back flat against
the trampoline, she asked: 'Mum,
how did the sky turn blue?'

Eight years old, and it was still new:
the bedsheet over her head not yet frayed.
It's how I look at you.

'The sea and sky kissed.
Blue is the colour of love.'

Rising to her feet, she lifted her arms above her head
then jumped,
reaching out to touch it: love

out of arm's reach,
outside of her body,
her arms in the wingspan of a plane.

And in that moment, I knew
I had failed her.

POOLSIDE GOSSIP

Hippo-crites in bathing suits, we snorted
pool water from our noses as we read aloud
poems from all the Instagram poets we hated,
despite us coming from the same tragic lineage.

With dramatic pauses between each line, I laughed
as you read *She* poems from men
who knew nothing about women,
only that they were 'brave' and 'enough'
and that their hair smelled better than
three-dollar drugstore shampoo.

Then you read Sylvia Plath. We both paused.
A deserved minute of silence.
Our tongues rolled out from our mouths like twin red carpets,
because frankly what more is there to say
about that jaw-dropping, mythical,
sad genius creature?

'I'm going to make Sylvia Plath an Instagram account,'
I vowed. 'I'll take photos of tulips with their heads cut off.
Post passive-aggressive memes about Ted's love for astrology.
Take a selfie of me gardening in my sad English cow-life.'

Putting my snarky face to your snarky face,
I kissed you for every damn snarky thing you've ever said.

We were a match made in Hell.
Not even the people we burned alive
were worthy of our flame.

THE BIRTH OF VENUS

Naked on your bed, you arrange my legs
with the same aesthetic consideration
used to arrange the pictures on your wall.
Your Venus in Libra. Everything is art.
I once saw a Botticelli painting
hanging on the inside of your heart.

Draping my last name on the back of your chair
with your jeans, you crown me, rename me.
'Oh. My. God': First name, middle name, surname.
Three necklaces of drool coiled across my chest.
I am Fibonacci: ever-expanding.
Your custom-made royal thing.

Untangling, we pull philosophy over
our two wet bodies like a bath towel.
I begin. This might be my favourite part.

'Identity is the real disorder,' I declare on the podium
of your chest. 'Tis the thief of all joy'—
hanging on for dear life to a fact, a belief, a delusion
with the kind of monkey grip that make-shifts Heaven
into a flimsy circus tent.

You smile. I fall in.
I am a know-it-all who knows nothing.
Only that peace, like death,
comes only on the fall.

LION TAMER

You might have no idea of your power,
but I do because I know mine.

My wildcat-hair untangled in your
hands, now as fine as fish bones.
Fangs buried in my gums
like shards of softened sea-glass.

Patting the baby lions in my mouth, I release their
roars. Watch them become kings on your tongue.
Stalk between my legs. Prowl through my womb.
Bite my heart, your bottom lip.

I let out sighs as big as babies our bodies rock to sleep.
You stroke my belly out of roars.
I file my nails short. Yawning
as I splay my fingers blissfully out of fight.

You might have no idea of your power,
but I do because I know mine.

Once I was a lion running rings around men
with my eyes closed,
and now I jump through yours with mine open,
calmly through your fire.

OTHER WOMEN

I wouldn't dream of handing over
those other versions of me to love you.

None of those women
are good enough for you.

NEW DEFINITIONS

Like dogs sniffing out a bone, we followed
the sign on Palm Canyon Drive
that read *Library*.
It was not a library.

But tables of old men,
glass cabinets and the unmistakeable
stench of wee.

No books, only models
of Cahuilla history.
Had they meant *Museum?*

What other words had been exchanged
in our absence from the world?

How long had we been gone
buried in each other's bodies like books
that libraries were no more libraries?

I pondered this with your kiss
barcoded on the back of my neck
with my new favourite definition of me.

GLORY

I've seen God. I'm waiting for nothing.

I've seen him
standing in my doorway in all his glory
asking if I wanted coffee.
Jesus, Mary and Joseph.

He was exquisite—each frame.
A stained-glass shard
even holier in full bloom.

He was my beginning,
and he was my death, I knew.

He was the entire damn life of me
flashing before my eyes.

LIPSTICK KISSES

Eleven years old,
we practiced
perfect lipstick kisses
on napkins, on mirrors, our arms —
not knowing it was pointless.

They all end up a stain on a man's lips.
A smudge on a pillowcase.
A hot flush of sex.
Mess.

LITTLE BIRDS
Homage to Anaïs Nin.

Crushed into the nest of his sofa,
he thrusts

harder
when he hears a mother
arrive home with her kid
to the apartment next door

harder
when he hears them chattering
outside, turning the key.
I feel him growing

harder
inside me, making me moan
louder than I want to
like the sound a little bird makes
begging for worm,
and it makes me wonder

how many times as a girl
I'd heard these little birds
flying from out a woman's mouth
in an apartment next door

and smiled.

MESS

The light creeps in like guilt.
Our bodies untangle like two necklaces
I would watch my mother untangle,
sitting quietly on the edge of her bed
with more patience than she had with me.

My head was no different, I imagine telling her now.
My thoughts, tangled necklaces. Not snakes.
There was nothing in my chaos to be feared.
My head a jewellery box of delicate things
that liked to tangle together,
just like our two bodies now
separating simply.

I play the conversation in my head.
Your sudden moan interrupts. Smiling
as you scoop up the wetness dribbling down my leg
with your index finger, delighting
in my mess.

VINCENT VAN COCK

I want to dip your cock in paint and create
a new world. Draw new men with it.
Men with hearts as big as their paintbrushes.
Men whose backs bend over backwards for women
like palm trees arching an eternal paradise.
Lilith would've stayed.

Men with hands that never close into fists.
I'd paint them flat and open like seas,
empty but for energy to weave between
of the free woman who moves like a deer.
I'd paint over the shotguns.
A cock is already a shotgun.
Your art doesn't repeat itself. It refreshes on the hour.
Weather flowing brushstroke to brushstroke,
gliding like fish never caught, nor counted.

I want your vision in the eyes of all.
Your wisdom in vivacious vistas,
your parallel panoramas gridded into matrixes of possibility
like gingham sundress portals
opening the golden legs of goddesses.

I see the art of men through you —
only through you, and sometimes
it is enough to bear them.

OTHERWORLD

This was how I remembered you from the otherworld:
you were my fourth-birthday present: a toy koala
whose smile fell off in my hands the first day
I held it. Mine, two years later.

You were a hiccup from a tickle.
A picture book stained by my grubby toddler fingers.
The light beneath the door that looked like hope.

In our last life, I was a flower. You picked me.
A daisy-fresh girl twirled between your index finger
and thumb. Each night I'd watch you sleep from the vase
on your nightstand.
I made it five days.
Writing my goodbye note in the air
with the alphabet of aroma.

In this life, we have words.
One bottle in a sea of ages
filled with a message I wrote twelve lifetimes ago:
I will come back to love you in one form or another.
This time, inside this pale ribboned body
sashed across your left shoulder. You won.

I have carried you forever in my mind,
guarded in a speech bubble of golden armour.
You: my first thought.

HOOKED

We hang our hellos on the hooks of our goodbyes
like coats, preparing for the cold before the cold comes.

I squeeze the missing out of you like dirty dishwater.
My love looks positively sparkling on you. Tell me lover,
are we destined to miss more than we kiss?

I pull my body from yours.
A scratchy Velcro rip so sudden it startles you.
You watch my naked walk to the bathroom. My left side red
from shoulder to thigh—red where you used to be.
I even up the right in the shower. The steam,
my replacement lover.
You know I need something scalding to match you, babe.
Something volcanic.

Packing my last things up from the hotel dresser,
you sit at the table, reaching for your keys.
A sweet soprano jangle that defines the moment.
The clang of the triangle rings.

Lifting my coat from the hook, I linger in the doorway,
facing the draught like a clever compass.

I was once a very warm thing,
the *warmest*, and soon,
I shall be cold.

CITIES

There'll be no babies, just poems.
No rosy-ribboned daughter named Sylvia or Anaïs.
No heavy-browed boy called Hemingway,
but Helvetica or Arial with a straight pageboy bob.
A Didot or a Georgia with curled serif eyelashes.

We won't be married on paper.
I won't take your last name. Just a pseudonym
to write nasty poems about you
when our inkwell runs dry.

We'll be a poem: one name at the bottom.
Never side by side on a power bill,
despite the electricity dancing at our fingertips.

We'll be buried in different cities,
but I loved you all over the place like rain.
Everywhere the rain fell,
I fell for you.

G R O C E R Y S T O R E

Taking turns to orient,
I lift my hand from your face
and arrow it to worlds
that hold us longer
than a week at a time.

I believe in worlds so bold
we only say goodbye
to go to the grocery store.

BIRD

I deserved you once by accident,
then perhaps, not again.
But I have patience to earn you.
I'd draw all 78 cards of Tarot for a chance
to re-spin our Wheel of Fortune.

We come and go like planets. *Mercury.*
Four times a year I spin in your hands.
These are the best times of my life.
It's like taking a shot of tequila.
It's like fitting in love all at once.

I am alone, but I am not lonely.
Loneliness lives in people you live with
that stop feeling like home. Old sweaters
the years bite holes the size of windows
you watch the rest of your sad little life through.

In between, there's airports.
I wait for the stewards to remember me by name.
Ask me if I ever get tired of flying.
And I will answer: 'Ask that to a bird.'

A SUN HALO OVER TINSELTOWN

Arms stretched across continents.
Worn thin. The heel of a sock.

I have an atlas in my palms.
My left open to America.
Cancer sun 22°.
I am the star-spangled dream.
My astrological coordinates: flecks of ash
from a cigarette thrown in the Mojave Desert.

A madman on a West Hollywood street corner
told me I looked like an angel from Heaven.
Begging passers-by to share his vision
as he pointed angelic accusations at me.
I ran like the devil.

God put us in a sock and shook us like dice.
Skipping three seas. Our lucky number up.
I lay flat on my back. A sailor's wheel.
Arms wide, legs apart, trying to reach you.

But don't you ever feel sorry for me.
Loving this large doesn't make me tragic, baby.
It makes me a star.

HOME SWEET HOME

The pictures hung like eyes
following me through the room.

Your lamps threw shade.
Your sheets undressed me.

The bamboo plant on your kitchen counter
breathed me in and made me new.

I was with you—in your home
and everything you owned
watched you inhabit me.

DEAR LIFE

Climbing into bed with our books for the night
we smile, amused
by the sweet ordinariness of it all.

Reading Louise Glück, you listen with your eyes closed.
My tongue a cicatrix of papercuts.
There is no bigger love-hate relationship
than one with a man who has better books than you.

You said you weren't feeling her.
That her words, although beautiful, were like fallen arrows
at your feet.
Could the soft bow of my voice make them fly? Could I try?
You thought hearing her in my voice might make something
click. Sentences connect like press studs. An accent
to shake the words up in your head like a snow dome.

Watching your eyes open, you slowly smiled.
I'd always wondered what an epiphany looked like.
Making her make sense to you, the way you do
the world for me.

When I tell you, my lover,
that I hang on your every word, I mean it.
For dear life.

GODS

You wrote me into your bedroom.
A master noun on legs
walking among your
people, places, and things.

A verb pulling out the adjectives between
my legs: *wet, warm, delicious*
as I sigh in perfect sentences
with the kind of eloquence
one could only expect from a sigh.

I could stay up all my life listening to you.
Licking your mouth for words. Sucking syllables
from your lips like stolen kisses.
I am fluent in you.
You are the conversation I've been dying to have.

You and me, don't you know,
we are gods—on paper and in bed,
and everywhere else,
mortally ordinary.

SPECIFIC

The romance of my conception feels superfluous somehow,
although admittedly, preferred.
I broke free from Mother first chance I got.
Gasping for an unshared breath. For a breath
not inside another breath.

Now I live in you. A light needs a lantern.
Your love contains me, and I seek containment.
A controlled flame that won't rip like wildfire.
A rage your rage snuffs out faster than a cigarette butt
on a boot heel.

They called me *Spitfire* as a kid.
My temper was famous. My tantrums, a favourite
dinner table recollection.
My mother would try to hold me—I'd scream.
But I prefer to believe I liked to be held.
I've gotten a lot of second opinions.

The optimists say love is abundant,
love is free. That it is everywhere, in everything,
but I disagree.
I've never known anything quite so specific.

D E N D R O C H R O N O L O G Y

You lived inside me all Summer,
like a child playing hide-and-seek
in the hollow of an oak tree.

Each hour, a new ring was drawn.
I counted them as you slept,
like a wife counts wedding anniversaries.

I aged thirty years in your bed.
My body almost gave up. Skin
puckered like grapes, dragged
from my bones with your teeth.

I became wine.
Red-stained with life and death like a placenta.
That intoxicating mix that makes you do
reckless things,
but I could care less.
A loved thing never cares if it's liked.

IN MY DREAMS I RUN SLOWLY

It was like some porn/thriller/slasher film you watch
with one eye open,
only mine were both open.

All eyes on me, watching me run into you
like I was being chased down by a murderer.
Like your heart was a store that closes at 9 and it was 8:55.
Like I had never found safe arms to run into —
which technically is bullshit,
but have you ever had a calm conversation
with a vagus nerve?

Running into you knowing you were already occupied.
That you had paintings on your wall,
plants in their corners to water,
a whole other life that existed before I kissed you,
before stapling mine to yours like an overachieving schoolgirl.
That you were ready for this.
That you were happy.

Truth is: I didn't notice.
I was just so damn hungry for you I suctioned my mouth
to your mouth like a barnacle,
sucking you up like meat from the bones
of your A-frame home.

Everyone else had reminded me of him, him, him —
except you, you, *you,*

and I wanted to know —
told myself I *deserved* to know a love
that made me forget what hate felt like.

A desperate woman is a dangerous woman.
All teeth. All bite.
A wolf in pearls.

In settled dust, I wonder what might've happened
had I walked into you slowly.
If I had wandered into your house,
saw your pictures on the walls,
the plants in their corners to be watered,
her holding onto your forearm the way I do now and said
simply, a lump of sugar in my throat:
'What a lovely home you have.'

If only I'd strolled
like I had twenty more places to go
after you. Visited like a guest bringing a cinnamon tea cake
in their hands instead of a grenade.
Walked past your numbered door,
your tree-lined street,
your history, and not thumbed through —
would you now have so many pages in your story
missing?

THE LOVER

I read *The Lover* on my last flight over to you.
A little French book
tucked in all the right places
like a pinafore. Reading it all the way through
front to back, the way my lips read you.
Speeding through lines. My eyes, two hungry mouths.
Love in verses dripping down my chin.

The lights went down in the cabin: the artificial dusk.
The passenger beside me rising to another seat. His broken,
no recline. Smiling into my page at my fortune,
I popped the LA lights like pills.
I didn't want to breathe in another man
before I breathed in you.

Two lovers. At first sight, linked.
They can't be together, just like we can't be together.
Meeting in pit stops, unwrapping love like a kebab
to eat on the go, burning our tongues on
takeaway coffee.
No time to take it slow.

The night of my departure, I leave the book in your bedroom
in lieu of me,
face to face, planting a kiss
on the book you're midway through.
I judge the cover. It's not about lovers.

I tell myself I want to pack light.
This softcover book of 128 pages,
suddenly too heavy.

I leave it like I left my toothbrush leaning against yours
in the cup, hoping one morning in a sleepy oblivion
you will use by mistake.
Two days later you tell me you did.
You said it was no mistake.

Weeks pass, I still wonder of the book.
Whether you've had time to read it—if so,
did you let it drip?
Did you read it more slowly than I did?
Let the words plant in your cheeks?
Let the story grow on you like a five o'clock shadow?

Instead, I bite my tongue.
I think of the title: *The Lover.*
Not lovers.
There is only one.

LYING DOWN

And so, it happened.
This great big wedge between us,
like a diving board in a Slim Aarons photograph.

No water to dive in, only tarmac.
Poisoned by that virus dripping down
the Western Pacific seas.

I could knock out my two front teeth
trying to get closer to you. I could break both my legs
trying to force things,
but it will only end in bruises.
It will only end in nowhere closer to you.

Still, this morning I tried.
Beating my fist into the heart I had
before the one in my chest grew
that fell in love with you. Trying to break everything
with a hairline crack in it.
I do like a finished thing.
But the wedge is sour, the carpel of an orange.
I can see at least nine more the same.

'How badly do you want this?' I hear the world ask.
'You are going to have to fight for it.
Just not how you usually do.
This fight you'll have to take lying down.'

ECLIPSE

The lamps suspect me.
Your pictures look at me cross-eyed. I wince
as your shadow bumps into me in the hallway.
I can hold my own.

Once I won a staring contest with the moon.
Not since you. Sadness makes me look down at my hands,
too proud of what I am carrying.

My ghost curves into your back when you sleep.
Crescent, never full.
I, who should've been gone 29.5 days ago.
I shush the mountains from your window looming
with their righteousness.
I won't listen to a thing that arches but begs for nothing.

This begging must count for something
bigger than my love that spends its days arguing with time:
Why would something as infinite as sand
be used to fill an hourglass?
But I've never understood the concept of irony.
Irony is just the human way of trying to explain an eclipse.
Something that feels right that shifts.

We met briefly for moments, then left,
but I never did.
Watch me overshadow you.

AIR STRIKE

All the planes grounded, so I flew
from my couch and into the air
like something suddenly too hot,
I could not bear it: to sink my toes
into the same dirt the plane wheels rolled in.
If they would not fly, then I would.

So, watch me now, rising in the air like steam.
My skin separated into a dust storm where all my sex goes up.
Keep your eyes to the sky, I'm rolling in like thunder.
My ten pins of reason knocked down.
The great air strike.

I am in front of you, can you see me?
Love without a birdlike neck to rest in the nest of your hands.
Love without a woman's body to store your collectibles
of manhood in.
Love without a kiss stamped to the inside of your wrists.

I am nothing but air.
But I am not nothing.

PANDEMIC OF LONELINESS

I might've helped keep people alive,
but I aged ten years without you.

I might've helped well people stay well,
but I was not well.

When this is over, I vow selfishness.
The kind of ruthless grab
with elbows as pointed as their question.
'*No*—it did not bring me enough satisfaction
to be good.'

Some days the ache was so big,
I wished them all dead.

PAPER PLANES

I will return to you different.
Missing you has changed me.

I no longer soften like butter beneath
the moon—I glare at it. Demand to know
how many cycles spin between us.
Peg Dali clockfaces on the clothesline to melt time.

My love has grit in it. It has spit.
It knows that shade of blue that leans into black,
like a hairline crack that hope leaks into.

I know what it's like to not have you
in a world I could always have you.

Heaven's gate: a closed border.
The City of Angels: a dusty desert bunker
of folded airplane wings,
like wishful origami
waiting to become different things.

TWELVE HOUSES

This is our last show. The third act.
You always liked me dressed in velvet,
draped over your lap like the final curtain.

We were born in a wheel of promise.
In the first house, it took merely a breath
to declare ourselves a miracle. In the fourth,
our mothers broke the hearts they made,
but we're all critical of our art.

I keep the bad reviews pinned to my memory.
Birth certificate, death notice
rolled together in a single scroll.
You and I graduating with honours.
My soul, your soul. *Namaste.*

Thank you for saving the last dance for me, Fred Astaire.
We twirled together through
all twelve houses of Pluto
and still never got used to the cold.

WISH YOU WERE HERE

Mills, Point Leo, Half Moon Bay.
Hermosa, Venice, Marina del Rey.
Blueprints of seas sent to each other's screens.
'Wish you were here.'

We meet in the sky in our dreams.
I count days like calories.
Never completely fed. Always hungry for you.

I cry too much.
'Big waves make for exciting surfing,' you soothe
when I apologise for my moods.
I want to lick your mouth like ice-cream
until I'm sick, sick of you.

I catch the end of your sigh, like a feather,
and look for our bird that's flown
to a moment in the distance
we can only picture with our eyes closed.

I want to kiss you like footsteps.
Amble over your skin, my big sexy risk.
I keep maps of you folded in my heart.
I always find my way back to you.

On 19 March 2020, the Prime Minister of Australia, Scott Morrison, announced the closure of Australia's borders as an emergency response to the COVID pandemic. After 262 days in lockdown, Melbourne became the longest locked-down city in the world. At times imposing overnight curfews from 9pm, residents could leave for up to an hour a day to exercise, and another to conduct essential, approved, services. On 1 November 2021, the borders re-opened. Most of us emerged well, yet most of us were broken.

Printed in Great Britain
by Amazon

41866173R00057